ISBN 1-58330-839-3

FELDHEIM PUBLISHERS
JERUSALEM   NEW YORK

POB 35002 / Jerusalem, Israel

202 Airport Executive Park
Nanuet, NY 10954

www.feldheim.com
Printed in Eretz Israel

Shikufitzky 3

written and illustrated by Shifra Glick

There are lots of stories in this book:
Some long, some short. Just take a look!
A color change of the border makes it clear
That a new story starts right here.

I can make the dolly fall,
Down to the porch below!
Now I'll drop a rubber ball.
It's fun to watch it go.

Teddy won't go through the bars,
Though I push with all my might.
I'll go get some little cars -
They should go through all right.

I found a book, a bottle, socks -
So many things to use!
Yiska's pink jewelry box,
A pair of Mommy's shoes.

This game is great! I love it! Wow!
It's so much fun to do.
But where's my pacifier now?
Did I really drop it too?!

16

The wonderful sister

by Temima Shikufitzky

Esti →  ← Rochi

Once opon a time there was a girl called Rochi, and she had a sister called Esti.

Esti never yelled at Rochi or called her names

You're so silly!

She always let Rochi use her things

Of corse you can use my new markers!

And she also helped her

Today I'm washing the dishes insted of you!

24

31

I don't know what to draw. Do you have any ideas, Kehos?

Draw our house.

That's our house?! But we don't have a yard, or a chimney, or a steep roof like that, or two windows over the door...It doesn't look like our house at all.

You're right, but I don't know how to draw an apartment on the third floor of a big building.

44

I've just got to remember what I wanted to say! It's driving me crazy! It's right on the tip of my tongue. I just know it was something very important!

I think you mentioned your teacher before Kehos interrupted. Maybe it was something about her.

That's right! Now I remember!

Nu, so tell me already! What was it?

Never mind. It's not all that important.

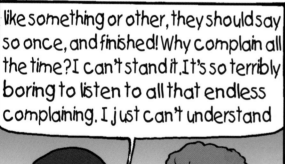

Temima's notebook doesn't look right.
Some color would make it more lively and bright.

I'll use my red crayon, yes, now a bit more...
There! It's much nicer than it was before.

Red and yellow, so pretty to see!
Temima will be so grateful to me.

I did her a favor –
I'm such a good boy!
So how come she isn't quite
Jumping for joy?

We're having a big test tomorrow, and three girls are coming to study with Chani.

Should I join them? Maybe I'll do better by myself. But sometimes studying in a group is easier... Mommy, tell me what to do!

I can't decide for you. You know these girls; you know how well you understand the subject. You need to think it over and make up your own mind.

But then I won't have anyone to blame if in the end I don't do well on the test!

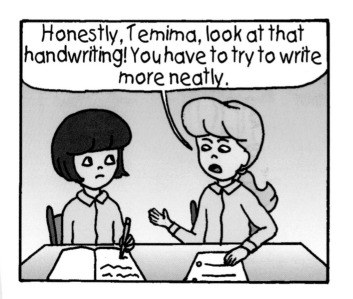

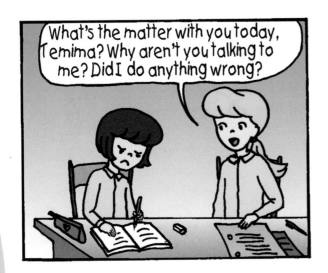

Yiska, did you notice that Sari came to school today with a braid instead of her ponytail?

Oh, Chani, you too? I'm sick of all this talk about Sari!

It's ridiculous! Why hang on Sari's every word, and copy everything she does?

It's so silly how the girls buy sandals just like Sari's, and decorate their notebooks the same way she does... like a flock of sheep, with no taste of their own!

The next day

Good morning, Yiska! You look different... Why did you braid your hair today?

Oh, I – I just felt like trying out a different hairstyle...

58

The next day:

Yiska, look what I drew! Isn't it pretty?

Leave me alone, Temima! I haven't got time to look at your drawing. I haven't got time to say: "It's very nice."

I don't even have time to say: "Yes"! Every second now is precious. We're having a very hard test tomorrow, and I haven't studied even half the stuff yet. And you come showing me pictures?

I can't look at anything now, do you understand? I don't have even one single second to spare!

I love making pretty decorations.
Our Sukka will be a beautiful sight!

I love looking up through the leafy
green S'chach
At the stars' shiny, silvery light.

I love to help with
building the Sukka,
Hammering in each nail
just right.

I love Simchas Torah – dancing up high!
Daddy, hold on to me tight!

Whenever I look out of my window I see the same old view. It's boring. I wish it would snow! Then the scene would change completely.

It would become magically beautiful! The cars, the fences – everything would be covered with a soft blanket of white.

I could play in the snow! Throw snowballs, make snowmen, till my fingers froze and my toes hurt terribly...

Yes, snow is wonderful. There's only one thing wrong with it – it's cold.

I love collecting interesting stuff.
It seems like I never can get enough:
Seashells, used phone-cards, rocks and sticks,
And a broken camera I just might fix.

Among my treasures there also are
Wheels that came off an old toy car,
Bottle caps, batteries, lockless keys,
Pens that **used** to write with ease,

A "binocular" (– broken half of a pair)
And a rubber stamp that's no longer all there.

Before Pesach Mommy threw everything out.
But I found something to be glad about –

My drawers are empty now – what a pleasure!
There's room to start storing lots of **new** treasure!

91

92

Temima, remember when we went to Meron on Lag Ba'Omer, when Kehos was three years old?

Oh yes, it was beautiful. There were so many people there, and a band, and dancing, and lots of three-year-olds who came to get their first haircut.

And the fathers danced with the little boys on their shoulders... and they cut off Kehos' long curls, and—

Hey, what's going on here? It's not fair! Everyone's talking about my Upsherin, and only I myself don't remember it at all.

Shavuos is a time for eating
Cheesecake and blintzes, it's true.

And filling the house with flowers
Of every fragrance and hue.

But more than that – it's for studying
Torah the whole night through,

For Shavuos is when the Torah
Was given to me and you!

Books that are worth buying

'cause you read them over and over and over again,
and have fun every single time!